MW00440404

NOTHING IS IMPOSSIBLE WITH GOD

A Christmas Devotional for Families

RICHARD A. ILES

WINTERS
PUBLISHING

Nothing Is Impossible With God

Copyright © 2019 by Richard A. Iles

All rights reserved. No part of this book may be reproduced in any form, except for brief quotations in reviews, without the written permission of the Author or Publisher.

Cover Design: Michael Iles (Author's son)
Page Design: Jake Moore (Author's son-in-law)

All Scripture quotations are taken from the *HOLY BIBLE, NEW INTERNATIONAL VERSION*®, *NIV*®, Copyright © 1973, 1978, 1984, 2011 by Biblica, Inc.® Used by permission of Zondervan. All rights reserved worldwide.

Published by Winters Publishing
www.winterspublishing.com
812-663-4948

Printed in the United States of America

ISBN: 978-1-883651-96-1

Library of Congress Control Number: 2019953001

To my children and grandchildren. I pray that you will love Jesus, the greatest gift ever given.

TABLE OF CONTENTS

TABLE OF CONTENTS

INTRODUCTION

When our children were between the ages of 5 and 10 years old, we searched for a devotional to use during Advent. We wanted them to envision the miraculous spiritual events which happened, and we wanted them to feel the remarkable human emotions and reactions that took place as this incredible story began to unfold. We also wanted a book which had some questions which could be used each day to help start a conversation about what we had read that day. We couldn't find anything we liked, and thus, the idea for this book was born.

The book is designed for one chapter to be read each day during the month of December. Read Chapter 1 on December 1, read Chapter 2 on December 2, etc. Read the Scripture verses, read the narrative, and ask the questions which you feel are appropriate for your family.

We have found that the book can be used by adults as well as by children. It has been used by adult Sunday school classes, by small groups, and even for personal devotions. We trust that this book will bring this wonderful story to life as you celebrate the first Advent of Jesus the Messiah.

Isaiah 7:10-14 | Again the LORD spoke to Ahaz, "Ask the LORD your God for a sign, whether in the deepest depths or in the highest heights."

But Ahaz said, "I will not ask; I will not put the LORD to the test."

Then Isaiah said, "Hear now, you house of David! Is it not enough to try the patience of humans? Will you try the patience of my God also? Therefore the Lord himself will give you a sign: The virgin will conceive and give birth to a son, and will call him Immanuel."

Micah 5:2 | But you, Bethlehem Ephrathah, though you are small among the clans of Judah, out of you will come for me one who will be ruler over Israel, whose origins are from of old, from ancient times.

Matthew 1:22-23 | All this took place to fulfill what the Lord had said through the prophet: "The virgin will conceive and give birth to a son, and they will call him Immanuel" (which means "God with us").

Many Old Testament Scriptures tell about God's son who would come to earth. They are called prophecies.

1

Although written many years before the son was born, they tell many things about his life and ministry. They also tell us many things about the birth of this son: the place, the special way he was to be born, his family tree, and even his name.

One of these Scriptures, Isaiah 7:10-14, states that Christ would be born of a virgin. (His mother would not have a baby the same way another woman would have a baby. The baby would not have a human father.) It also tells us that his mother would give him a special name. This name would be Immanuel which means "God with us." This promised baby would be a human baby, but he would also be God. This baby was God, and he chose to become a human baby so he could come to earth and live and die for our sins.

Another Scripture, Micah 5:2, tells that Christ would be born in the city of Bethlehem. When the religious leaders were asked by Herod where the King would be born, they quoted him this Scripture and said, "In Bethlehem." These religious leaders who were alive when Jesus was born knew where the promised King would be born, knew he would be born of a virgin, and knew what he would be named. They knew because of Old Testament prophecies.

From now until Christmas, we will see many ways in which Old Testament prophecies were fulfilled by the baby named Immanuel who was born in Bethlehem of the virgin Mary (Matthew 1:22-23).

Questions for Discussion

1. What is Prophecy?
2. What is a virgin? (Children will probably ask this.)
3. How can Jesus be human and God at the same time?
4. Why did Jesus come to earth as a baby?
5. Why do you think God gave us a description of the King before he was born?
6. Why didn't the religious leaders believe Jesus was the Savior when they knew he was supposed to be born?

Summary Note

The Old Testament prophecies about the son have only been fulfilled by one person in all of history— Jesus, the babe in the manger, the Savior of the world.

DECEMBER 2 | Lineage of Abraham and David

(Explain that the verses from Matthew and Luke are records of a family tree. Don't read them verse by verse. Name some of the people who are mentioned here.)

Matthew 1:1-17 | This is the genealogy of Jesus the Messiah the son of David, the son of Abraham:
Abraham was the father of Isaac,
Isaac the father of Jacob,
Jacob the father of Judah and his brothers,
Judah the father of Perez and Zerah, whose mother was Tamar,
Perez the father of Hezron,
Hezron the father of Ram,
Ram the father of Amminadab,
Amminadab the father of Nahshon,
Nahshon the father of Salmon,
Salmon the father of Boaz, whose mother was Rahab,
Boaz the father of Obed, whose mother was Ruth,
Obed the father of Jesse,
and Jesse the father of King David.

David was the father of Solomon, whose mother had been Uriah's wife,
Solomon the father of Rehoboam,

Rehoboam the father of Abijah,

Abijah the father of Asa,

Asa the father of Jehoshaphat,

Jehoshaphat the father of Jehoram,

Jehoram the father of Uzziah,

Uzziah the father of Jotham,

Jotham the father of Ahaz,

Ahaz the father of Hezekiah,

Hezekiah the father of Manasseh,

Manasseh the father of Amon,

Amon the father of Josiah,

and Josiah the father of Jeconiah and his brothers at the time of the exile to Babylon.

After the exile to Babylon:

Jeconiah was the father of Shealtiel,

Shealtiel the father of Zerubbabel,

Zerubbabel the father of Abihud,

Abihud the father of Eliakim,

Eliakim the father of Azor,

Azor the father of Zadok,

Zadok the father of Akim,

Akim the father of Elihud,

Elihud the father of Eleazar,

Eleazar the father of Matthan,

Matthan the father of Jacob,

and Jacob the father of Joseph, the husband of Mary, and Mary was the mother of Jesus who is called the Messiah.

Thus there were fourteen generations in all from Abraham to David, fourteen from David to the exile to Babylon, and fourteen from the exile to the Messiah.

Luke 3:23-38 | Now Jesus himself was about thirty years old when he began his ministry. He was the son, so it was thought, of Joseph,

the son of Heli, the son of Matthat,
the son of Levi, the son of Melki,
the son of Jannai, the son of Joseph,
the son of Mattathias, the son of Amos,
the son of Nahum, the son of Esli,
the son of Naggai, the son of Maath,
the son of Mattathias, the son of Semein,
the son of Josek, the son of Joda,
the son of Joanan, the son of Rhesa,
the son of Zerubbabel, the son of Shealtiel,
the son of Neri, the son of Melki,
the son of Addi, the son of Cosam,
the son of Elmadam, the son of Er,
the son of Joshua, the son of Eliezer,
the son of Jorim, the son of Matthat,
the son of Levi, the son of Simeon,

the son of Judah, the son of Joseph,
the son of Jonam, the son of Eliakim,
the son of Melea, the son of Menna,
the son of Mattatha, the son of Nathan,
the son of David, the son of Jesse,
the son of Obed, the son of Boaz,
the son of Salmon, the son of Nahshon,
the son of Amminadab, the son of Ram,
the son of Hezron, the son of Perez,
the son of Judah, the son of Jacob,
the son of Isaac, the son of Abraham,
the son of Terah, the son of Nahor,
the son of Serug, the son of Reu,
the son of Peleg, the son of Eber,
the son of Shelah, the son of Cainan,
the son of Arphaxad, the son of Shem,
the son of Noah, the son of Lamech,
the son of Methuselah, the son of Enoch,
the son of Jared, the son of Mahalalel,
the son of Kenan, the son of Enosh,
the son of Seth, the son of Adam,
the son of God.

Genesis 12:1-3 | The LORD had said to Abram, "Go from your country, your people and your father's household to the land I will show you. I will make you into a great nation, and I will bless you; I will make your name great, and you will be a blessing. I will bless those who bless you, and whoever curses you I will curse; and all peoples on earth will be blessed through you."

2 Samuel 7:12-13 | "When your days are over and you rest with your ancestors, I will raise up your offspring to succeed you, your own flesh and blood, and I will establish his kingdom. He is the one who will build a house for my Name, and I will establish the throne of his kingdom forever." *(This is God speaking to David.)*

The ancestors of Christ included many godly and interesting men and women. Among them were Abraham, Ruth, David, Solomon, and Hezekiah. These men and women were spiritual people who depended on God to lead them. They were men and women who desired to do God's will.

Abraham was chosen by God to be the father of a new nation. Also, he was chosen to be one of the ancestors of Christ—the Savior of the world. Even when he had grown very old Abraham continued to believe God's message that he would have a son. He had looked forward to the birth of this son for many years so that he was overjoyed when his wife gave birth to Isaac. Abraham remained faithful when God asked him to sacrifice his son on an altar. He was willing to do all that God asked of him, even if it meant giving up his son (see Genesis 15:1-6 and 21:1-22:19).

Ruth was a Moabite woman married to a man from Israel. When her husband died, Ruth faithfully stayed with her mother-in-law accepting the Israelites as her people and their God as her God. This choice brought her the blessing of both a new husband and a son. Through her son Ruth became the great-grandmother of David, an ancestor of Christ.

David was a godly man whom God used in a mighty way when he was young. David defended the whole army against Goliath and defeated him with one small stone. He entered this fight by saying, "I come against you in the name of the Lord Almighty" (1 Samuel 17:45). David depended on God for strength and power to win such a great victory (see 1 Samuel 17:1-58).

Solomon started his leadership of the nation by asking God to give him wisdom to know how to rule and judge his people. He put the needs of his people before his own needs and wants. God gave him wisdom and everything else he desired, because he unselfishly asked for the greatest gift a king could receive: wisdom to rule his people well (see 1 Kings 3:1-15).

Hezekiah, at the age of twenty-five, became king when the nation was worshipping false gods. He cleansed the temple, got rid of false priests and gods, and reopened the temple to true worship of God. When he was going to die, he asked God to extend his life, so God gave him fifteen more years to live. He was a man who determined that he would serve God (see 2 Kings 20:1-11).

These men and women were ancestors of Christ. Their stories had been told for hundreds of years to children in the Jewish nation. Once again they would be told to a child, the Christ child, by his mother and father, both of whom were of the lineage of David.

Questions for Discussion

1. What is a family tree?
2. Which man or woman do you think is the most interesting? Why?
3. Do you know any other stories about these men or women?
4. God promised Abraham all nations would be blessed through his family. How would this happen?
5. Do you know any interesting facts about a godly man or woman in your family tree?

Summary Note

The Old Testament promised that Christ would have Abraham and David as his ancestors, and the New Testament begins by telling us this is exactly what happened.

DECEMBER 3 | Angelic Appearance to Zechariah

Luke 1:5-25 | In the time of Herod king of Judea there was a priest named Zechariah, who belonged to the priestly division of Abijah; his wife Elizabeth was also a descendant of Aaron. Both of them were righteous in the sight of God, observing all the Lord's commands and decrees blamelessly. But they were childless because Elizabeth was not able to conceive, and they were both very old.

Once when Zechariah's division was on duty and he was serving as priest before God, he was chosen by lot, according to the custom of the priesthood, to go into the temple of the Lord and burn incense. And when the time for the burning of incense came, all the assembled worshipers were praying outside.

Then an angel of the Lord appeared to him, standing at the right side of the altar of incense. When Zechariah saw him, he was startled and was gripped with fear. But the angel said to him: "Do not be afraid, Zechariah; your prayer has been heard. Your wife Elizabeth will bear you a son, and you are to call him John. He will be a joy and delight to you, and many will rejoice because of his birth, for he will be great in the sight of the Lord. He is never to take wine or other fermented drink, and he will be filled with the Holy Spirit even before he is born. He will bring back many of the people of Israel to the Lord their God. And he will go on before the Lord, in the spirit and power of Elijah, to turn the hearts of the parents to their children and the disobedient to the wisdom of the righteous—to make ready a people prepared for the Lord."

Zechariah asked the angel, "How can I be sure of this? I am an old man and my wife is well along in years."

The angel said to him, "I am Gabriel. I stand in the presence of God, and I have been sent to speak to you and to tell you this good news. And now you will be silent and not able to speak until the day this happens, because you did not believe my words, which will come true at their appointed time."

Meanwhile, the people were waiting for Zechariah and wondering why he stayed so long in the temple. When he came out, he could not speak to them. They realized he had seen a vision in the temple, for he kept making signs to them but remained unable to speak.

When his time of service was completed, he returned home. After this his wife Elizabeth became pregnant and for five months remained in seclusion. "The Lord has done this for me," she said. "In these days he has shown his favor and taken away my disgrace among the people."

It was the time of the morning sacrifice. A priest named Zechariah had been chosen to offer the sacrifice. This was a very special honor. He would only get to do this one time in his whole life. He was to go into the Holy Place in the temple and burn incense to God.

Zechariah moved to the altar and spread the incense, but as he did so he noticed an angel standing by the altar. He was afraid and could not speak. The angel, as directed by God, told Zechariah a heavenly message. First of all, the angel said that the prayer of Zechariah would be answered: a Savior would be born into this world. Second, the angel said that another prayer had been answered: Zechariah's wife, Elizabeth, would have a son. Finally, the angel told Zechariah some interesting facts about his unborn son:

1. He would be named John.
2. He would be great.
3. He would be a Nazarite.
4. He would be filled with the Holy Spirit.
5. He would be the forerunner of Christ.

Zechariah finally mustered the courage to speak, but with doubt in his heart, he asked for a sign from the angel to show this was truly a God-sent message. So the angel gave him an unexpected sign: he made him dumb, unable to speak.

Zechariah was supposed to step out of the Holy Place and say a prayer before the people. He came out, stood silently, tried to speak and couldn't. The people knew by his silence and gestures that something had happened in the temple. They wondered: has this country priest had a vision from God? Indeed he had!

Questions for Discussion

1. What is incense?
2. Would you be afraid if an angel appeared to you? Why or why not?
3. Why did Zechariah ask for a sign to prove that the angel's message was true?
4. Would you have believed the angel? Why or why not?
5. What did it mean that John would be great, would be filled with the Holy Spirit, and would be the forerunner of Christ?
6. Does God still answer prayer? What can we learn about prayer from this story?

Summary Note

The announcement to Zechariah that his prayer was answered and that his son would be forerunner of Christ was an announcement that soon Christ would come to the earth.

DECEMBER 4 | Angelic Appearance to Mary

Luke 1:26-38 | In the sixth month of Elizabeth's pregnancy, God sent the angel Gabriel to Nazareth, a town in Galilee, to a virgin pledged to be married to a man named Joseph, a descendant of David. The virgin's name was Mary. The angel went to her and said, "Greetings, you who are highly favored! The Lord is with you."

Mary was greatly troubled at his words and wondered what kind of greeting this might be. But the angel said to her, "Do not be afraid, Mary; you have found favor with God. You will conceive and give birth to a son, and you are to call him Jesus. He will be great and will be called the Son of the Most High. The Lord God will give him the throne of his father David, and he will reign over Jacob's descendants forever; his kingdom will never end."

"How will this be," Mary asked the angel, "since I am a virgin?"

The angel answered, "The Holy Spirit will come on you, and the power of the Most High will overshadow you. So the holy one to be born will be called the Son of God. Even Elizabeth your relative is going to have a child in her old age, and she who was said to be unable to conceive is in her sixth month. Nothing is impossible with God."

"I am the Lord's servant," Mary answered. "May your word to me be fulfilled." Then the angel left her.

Six months after the angel appeared to Zechariah in the Holy Place he was sent on another mission. This time he was instructed to deliver a startling message to a young girl in the town of Nazareth. Her name was Mary. She was a virgin who was pledged to be married to a carpenter named Joseph. The angel had a special and unique message for her. He began by telling her she was highly favored by God. This message probably came as a shock to her. She may have wondered why God would favor her. The angel answered her unasked question by telling her she had been chosen for a special and unusual honor—she was going to have a baby, a son.

Immediately after telling Mary that God had chosen her for this special honor, the angel told her some amazing things about the child:

1. He would be named Jesus
2. He would be great.
3. He would be called the Son of the Highest.
4. He would be given the throne of his father David.
5. He would have an everlasting kingdom.

Mary was curious. She wanted to know how this could be possible. She believed it, but she wanted to know how God would make it happen. The angel told her that the Holy Spirit would come upon her and God's power would overshadow her. He reminded her that with God nothing is impossible. As she meditated on these words, the angel gave her an unasked-for sign—he told her that Elizabeth, her relative, was going to have a baby even though she was very old.

Mary was overjoyed at this great news and said, "I am the Lord's servant. May it be to me as you have said." She was excited and happy that God had chosen her to be the woman who would give birth to his son. Her reply showed that she was happy to do whatever God wanted her to do. She determined in her heart that she would be obedient to anything God would ask of her.

Questions for Discussion

1. Why did God chose Mary?
2. What does overshadow mean?
3. If an angel appeared to you and told you that you were special would you be curious and want to know why God had chosen you?
4. Do you think Mary was a good choice? Why or why not?
5. Is everything possible for God to do?
6. How did Mary show she was obedient?
7. Does God have a special plan for your life?
8. Are you ready to do whatever God asks you to do?

Summary Note

Mary was overjoyed and thankful that God had chosen her to be the woman who would give birth to his son. She was willing to be obedient to the leadership of God. As a result of this, she would be the mother of the son of God, the ruler of the world, the Savior of men.

DECEMBER 5 | Mary Visits Elizabeth

Luke 1:39-45 | At that time Mary got ready and hurried to a town in the hill country of Judea, where she entered Zechariah's home and greeted Elizabeth. When Elizabeth heard Mary's greeting, the baby leaped in her womb, and Elizabeth was filled with the Holy Spirit. In a loud voice she exclaimed: "Blessed are you among women, and blessed is the child you will bear! But why am I so favored, that the mother of my Lord should come to me? As soon as the sound of your greeting reached my ears, the baby in my womb leaped for joy. Blessed is she who has believed that the Lord would fulfill his promises to her!"

The day after the angel visited Mary she must have wondered if she had dreamed the whole thing. After all, wasn't it strange that she would be chosen for this great honor? Wasn't it impossible that she would have a baby? Hadn't the angel also told her that her elderly relative, Elizabeth, would have a child? She needed to talk to someone! While thinking about all that had happened and all she had been told, Mary decided that the perfect person to talk to was Elizabeth, the elderly woman who was going to have a son. Mary would share her miraculous story with another woman who was giving birth to a son in a miraculous way.

Since Mary could not make the trip to Zechariah and Elizabeth's alone, she went down to the well at daybreak and joined a caravan that was forming for a trip to Jerusalem. She would simply walk with them to the city of Jerusalem and then go on to the city where Zechariah and Elizabeth lived. This trip through Galilee, across the Jordan River, through Perea, back across the Jordan River, and up the steep road to Jerusalem, took four or five days and covered about eighty-five miles.

After arriving in Jerusalem, Mary took one of the southern roads and walked to the home of Zechariah and Elizabeth. When she arrived at the house, she stepped inside the door and called Elizabeth's name. At the sound of her voice, the Holy Spirit came to Elizabeth and told her what had happened to Mary. Even the baby inside of Elizabeth leaped for joy.

Elizabeth, inspired by the Holy Spirit, then blessed Mary three times.

1) "Blessed are you among women" (Luke 1:42). Mary was distinctively blessed, since she was selected to give birth to the Messiah of the nation.

Many women from the tribe of Judah would have loved to have been this chosen mother.

2) "Blessed is the child you will bear" (Luke 1:42). Zechariah surely must have told Elizabeth that their son was chosen to be the forerunner of the Messiah. Now, as she heard the message of the Holy Spirit, she understood that the child Mary would bear is the Messiah—the Savior that she, her husband, and the nation have prayed for.

3) "Blessed is she who has believed that what the Lord has said to her will be accomplished" (Luke 1:45). Mary was also blessed because she believed what the angel had told her. Elizabeth encouraged her by giving her a message from the Holy Spirit: what the Lord had said will be fulfilled.

Elizabeth, knowing she was the mother of the forerunner of the Christ, now meets the mother of the Messiah, and it causes great joy and gladness. Just as she knew the destiny of her son, she now knew that the advent of the Christ was very soon.

Questions for Discussion

1. Was Mary afraid that next morning when she thought about the angel's message? Why or why not?
2. Why was it such a long journey from Nazareth to the home of Zechariah and Elizabeth?
3. What does it mean that the Holy Spirit filled Elizabeth?
4. What does it mean that the baby leaped?
5. Why did the baby leap?
6. Mary was blessed because she believed God's message. Do you believe the message of God that we find in his book, the Bible?

Summary Note

The Holy Spirit revealed to Elizabeth that Mary, a virgin, was the fulfillment of Isaiah 7:14 (see day 1). This message from Elizabeth to Mary reassured Mary that she had indeed been chosen by God to give birth to the Messiah.

DECEMBER 6 | Mary's Song of Praise

Luke 1:46-56 | And Mary said:

> "My soul glorifies the Lord
> and my spirit rejoices in God my Savior,
> for he has been mindful
> of the humble state of his servant.
> From now on all generations will call me blessed,
> for the Mighty One has done great things for me—
> holy is his name.
> His mercy extends to those who fear him,
> from generation to generation.
> He has performed mighty deeds with his arm;
> he has scattered those who are proud in their
> inmost thoughts.
> He has brought down rulers from their thrones
> but has lifted up the humble.
> He has filled the hungry with good things
> but has sent the rich away empty.
> He has helped his servant Israel,
> remembering to be merciful
> to Abraham and his descendants forever,
> just as he promised our ancestors."

Mary stayed with Elizabeth for about three months and then returned home.

As Mary listened to the blessing of Elizabeth, she wondered how Elizabeth even knew that she was going to have a baby. No one could have told Elizabeth because Mary had not told anyone. She had left Nazareth immediately after the angel had appeared to her. She hadn't even told Joseph, her espoused husband, that she was going away. Her heart seemed to stop as she suddenly realized what Joseph must be going through as he scoured the town and the immediate hill country in search of his fiancé. However, the greeting of Elizabeth turned Mary's thoughts toward the message of the angel and the God who had sent him. Mary soon understood that Elizabeth knew because she was filled with the Holy Spirit. Elizabeth was speaking this blessing because the Holy Spirit had told her that Mary would be the mother of the Christ child.

As Mary reflected upon the mystery of the virgin birth and the blessing of Elizabeth, she burst forth in a song of praise to her holy God. In this song, called the Magnificat, Mary said that she was thrilled that God had chosen her to give birth to his son. She said that God had done great things for her and that throughout history people would remember her as one who was especially blessed by God. In this song she reminded Elizabeth that God was truly a Holy God who always kept his word and who was always merciful to his people. She remembered that God had been faithful to his promise to Abraham (see day 1) as she realized that she would be the mother of the child who would bring the promised blessing to all peoples of the earth. Mary praised God and his greatness, mercy, and love as she sang this song.

Finally, exhausted from the excitement of the hour, these two women fell into each other's arms and shared in silence the great things that God had done for them.

Questions for Discussion

1. How did Mary feel when Elizabeth blessed her?
2. What does it mean that God is holy?
3. What had God promised Abraham? Does God always keep his promises?
4. Do you remember to praise God for his blessings to you?

Summary Note

The mother of Christ and the mother of the forerunner of Christ had shared a very special time when they met and told each other all that God had done. Now they would spend several months together in preparation and joy of the expected births of their God-sent sons.

DECEMBER 7 | Birth of John and Praise of Zechariah

Luke 1:57-80 | When it was time for Elizabeth to have her baby, she gave birth to a son. Her neighbors and relatives heard that the Lord had shown her great mercy, and they shared her joy.

On the eighth day they came to circumcise the child, and they were going to name him after his father Zechariah, but his mother spoke up and said, "No! He is to be called John."

They said to her, "There is no one among your relatives who has that name."

Then they made signs to his father, to find out what he would like to name the child. He asked for a writing tablet, and to everyone's astonishment he wrote, "His name is John." Immediately his mouth was opened and his tongue set free, and he began to speak, praising God. All the neighbors were filled with awe, and throughout the hill country of Judea people were talking about all these things. Everyone who heard this wondered about it, asking, "What then is this child going to be?" For the Lord's hand was with him.

His father Zechariah was filled with the Holy Spirit and prophesied:

"Praise be to the Lord, the God of Israel,
because he has come to his people and redeemed
them.
He has raised up a horn of salvation for us
in the house of his servant David
(as he said through his holy prophets of long ago),
salvation from our enemies
and from the hand of all who hate us—
to show mercy to our ancestors
and to remember his holy covenant,
the oath he swore to our father Abraham:
to rescue us from the hand of our enemies,
and to enable us to serve him without fear
in holiness and righteousness before him all our
days.

"And you, my child, will be called a prophet of the
Most High;
for you will go on before the Lord to prepare the
way for him,
to give his people the knowledge of salvation
through the forgiveness of their sins,
because of the tender mercy of our God,
by which the rising sun will come to us from
heaven
to shine on those living in darkness
and in the shadow of death,

to guide our feet into the path of peace."

And the child grew and became strong in spirit; and he lived in the wilderness until he appeared publicly to Israel.

After sharing the special joy and happiness of the announcement of their expected births, Mary and Elizabeth spent the next three months together. Each day they probably talked about their unborn sons. They discussed how they were such special sons and how they would raise them. Each of them, in her own heart, thought about the special mission of her son. Each day they thanked God that they had been chosen to be the mothers of these special children.

Finally the day came when Elizabeth was going to give birth to her son. Her friends and relatives gathered outside her home to await the arrival of the child. When it was announced that she had given birth to a son, a great shout of joy rang out. Her friends and relatives shared her joy as they too thanked God for the extraordinary and safe birth of this beautiful child.

These same friends and relatives gathered at Zechariah and Elizabeth's home eight days later to escort them to the temple where the child would be circumcised and then named. The crowd was restless as they got their first look at the child and as they strained to hear Elizabeth tell the details of this birth. As this merry band traveled to the temple, they began to ask each other what the child would be named. The consensus was the he should be named Zechariah after his father. But Elizabeth said, "No! He is to be called John." "But why John?" the crowd asked. "You have no relatives by that name." Unable to understand her reasoning or change her mind, the crowd turned to Zechariah and asked him the same question. Zechariah, who still could not speak since being made dumb by the angel, motioned for a tablet and wrote "John." The crowd was startled, but this was only the beginning.

Immediately the silence of nine long months was broken. Zechariah could speak and speak he did! The Holy Spirit filled him with a most interesting and unbelievable message. First of all, Zechariah spoke to his friends and relatives. He reminded them that the Lord God of Israel had promised Abraham that he would raise a king from the house of David to redeem his people. This king would rescue Israel from their enemies and lead them in holy worship to the true God. Zechariah spoke to them as if this event had just recently occurred. Surely they were astonished and wondered about the accuracy of his words. Sensing the disbelief of the crowd, Zechariah directed his speech to his son and answered the crowd's questions. He proclaimed that John was the highest prophet who would go before the highest son—the Lord. Zechariah explained that John's mission was that of preparing the people to meet the Lord and that his message was the message of salvation.

The reaction of the crowd was one of wonder and fear as they asked this question among themselves, "What is this child going to be?" They realized that the hand of the Lord was with him.

Questions for Discussion

1. Why did they name the baby John?
2. What is circumcision? (Your child might ask this.)
3. What was John's mission?
4. What was John's message?
5. Why were the people afraid?
6. What does it mean that the hand of the Lord was with him?
7. How can you be like John and tell the world that Jesus is coming?

Summary Note

When John was born, Zechariah praised God because he now knew that soon Christ would be born. He looked forward to the day when his son would announce to the people that Christ their Savior was coming to teach them the way of salvation.

DECEMBER 8 | Mary's Return and Joseph's Dream

Matthew 1:18-25 | This is how the birth of Jesus the Messiah came about: His mother Mary was pledged to be married to Joseph, but before they came together, she was found to be pregnant through the Holy Spirit. Because Joseph her husband was faithful to the law, and yet did not want to expose her to public disgrace, he had in mind to divorce her quietly.

But after he had considered this, an angel of the Lord appeared to him in a dream and said, "Joseph son of David, do not be afraid to take Mary home as your wife, because what is conceived in her is from the Holy Spirit. She will give birth to a son, and you are to give him the name Jesus, because he will save his people from their sins."

All this took place to fulfill what the Lord had said through the prophet: "The virgin will conceive and give birth to a son, and they will call him Immanuel" (which means "God with us").

When Joseph woke up, he did what the angel of the Lord had commanded him and took Mary home as his wife. But he did not consummate their marriage until she gave birth to a son. And he gave him the name Jesus.

Mary had bid Elizabeth and her family farewell and now joined another caravan headed for Nazareth. Each step brought her nearer her family, friends and fiancé—Joseph. Each step became slower and heavier as she came up the hill and viewed the city where she had been raised. The joy of being the mother of the Messiah was now briefly forgotten as Mary thought about being accused of sinning, being rejected by her friends, the disappointment of her parents, the lack of understanding, and finally, the possible loss of her fiancé. She asked herself these questions: How would she explain? How could she face them? What would they think? What would Joseph do? Has God brought me from a house of joy to a house of hatred when they realize I am pregnant?

Mary made her way home and explained to her parents where she had been. Then, wanting Joseph and her parents to hear the news of her unborn son together, she had someone go find him to tell him she was back. She requested that he come to see her for she had some amazing news to share with him.

Joseph was found, and he ran to the house of Mary, anxious to see her and ask the questions which had filled his mind for the last three months. Where had she been? Why had she gone away? Was she alright? How could she leave without telling him? Why hadn't she even said goodbye? Had she sinned and left because of shame? Why had she done it? Before Joseph had a chance to ask any of these questions, Mary quietly greeted him and began to tell him what had happened in the last three months. She told him of the angelic appearance, the God-sent message, her trip to Elizabeth's, the blessing of Elizabeth, the birth of John, and the speech of Zechariah at John's circumcision. She concluded by reminding him that the child she now carried was the Christ child, the Savior of Israel.

Now Joseph's mind was filled with more questions: Should he believe this story? Had an angel really appeared? Or had she left with another man? What should he do? Should he divorce her privately or have her suffer the shame of a public divorce? After hearing the story, his head full of questions, anger and disbelief, Joseph ran from the house to his carpenter shop. As his head began to clear, he had only one final question—How could he break off the wedding plans without hurting the one who had probably sinned against him?

As Joseph spent a restless night thinking about the hard decision he must make, God in heaven summoned his angel again and instructed him to visit this troubled man. Early in the morning, after Joseph had finally fallen asleep, this angel appeared to him in a dream. The angel's heaven-sent message was simple—"Don't be afraid to marry Mary; her child is the child of God, conceived of the Holy Spirit." The angelic message proved to Joseph that the story of Mary was true. Joseph simply believed, and his mind was filled with a newfound peace.

The angel then told Joseph that the child was a boy, that he would be named Jesus, and that he would save his people from their sins. He reminded Joseph that the virgin-born son would be a fulfillment of Isaiah's prophecy given 700 years ago (see day 1). After delivering the message, the angel departed and left Joseph alone to think about this revelation from God. Joseph realized that God had given him guidance at a time when he needed to make a difficult decision, and he willingly obeyed the command he had been given—he took Mary to be his wife.

Questions for Discussion

1. Why was it hard for Mary to tell Joseph?
2. Did Joseph believe her before the angel appeared?
3. Why did God send the angel?
4. Should Joseph have divorced Mary?
5. Why didn't Joseph divorce Mary?
6. Would you have believed the angel?

Summary Note

Mary had come home secure in the fact that she would be the mother of Jesus, the Savior of his people. This security was made stronger as Joseph heard her story, followed the message of God, and took her home as his wife.

DECEMBER 9 | Traveling to Bethlehem

Luke 2:1-5 | In those days Caesar Augustus issued a decree that a census should be taken of the entire Roman world. (This was the first census that took place while Quirinius was governor of Syria.) And everyone went to their own town to register.

So Joseph also went up from the town of Nazareth in Galilee to Judea, to Bethlehem the town of David, because he belonged to the house and line of David. He went there to register with Mary, who was pledged to be married to him and was expecting a child.

The next three or four months must have been both difficult and wonderful as Mary and Joseph suffered the scorn of their neighbors yet shared the wonder that they would be the parents of the son of God. One day they heard people shouting as Roman soldiers rode into the city. Down near the well the soldiers posted a decree from the Emperor, Augustus. He had decided to take a census of his empire. Every man was to return to the city of his birth, be counted, and pay his taxes. As Mary and Joseph read this decree, they knew they must go to Bethlehem. Thinking back to the message of the angel, their promised son, and the nearness of his birth, they understood that God was moving the entire population of the country to get them to Bethlehem. They laughed and talked much about the way God worked in their lives and how he kept the promises of his prophecies.

To make this journey Mary and Joseph joined a large caravan of their neighbors who were also going to towns in Judea and Perea. Mary, about ready to give birth to her son, once again started on the trip she had taken several months ago when she had gone to visit Elizabeth. Spreading a blanket on the back of a donkey and using their belongings as a backrest, Joseph helped Mary onto the donkey, and they started on their journey. The first day's travel was the easiest day of the trip. However, after riding all day, Mary was exhausted. Her back was stiff and sore, and it seemed that every bone in her body ached. Joseph prepared a place for her to sleep and tried to make her as comfortable as possible. Due to her exhaustion, the soreness of her body, and the nearness of the birth of the baby, Mary tossed and turned all through the night.

The second and third days of the trip were especially hard on this young mother-to-be. Traveling through Perea was long, hot, and difficult. They stopped often so Joseph could give Mary a refreshing cup of water or try to make her more comfortable on the donkey. Again, Mary spent restless nights dreading the arrival of morning when she knew she must once again ride on the donkey. The baby began to cause a lot of discomfort, and she wondered if he might be born before they reached the town of Bethlehem.

Awakening early on the fourth morning Mary did not want to arise from her bed. She knew that this day's travel would be the most difficult. She dreaded the hours she would have to spend on the donkey as he made his way up the steep incline to Jerusalem. Joseph walked beside her and comforted her as they made this trip. He encouraged her by talking about seeing friends and relatives they had not seen for many years. He also reminded her of the plan of God—how God had put the special baby in her womb, had blessed her during her pregnancy, and was now leading them to Bethlehem where prophecy said the Christ would be born.

Having not quite reached the city by nightfall, Mary and Joseph found a place to camp and settled down for the night. That night Mary rested better than any other night of the trip. She rested well partly from total exhaustion and partly from knowing they would reach Bethlehem the next day. Morning came and they set off on the last part of their journey. As the caravan moved south of Jerusalem, Mary and Joseph noticed the countryside and remembered that their ancestor David had walked these hills and valleys as he watched his sheep. They remembered that it was in these hills that David had written many of his psalms and sang them to the Lord. Joseph cheered Mary by singing some of these psalms as they trod down the road toward the town of their ancestors.

As evening fell, the town of Bethlehem came into view. It was a beehive of activity. Mary and Joseph could see many people pouring into the city on each road that led to it. Knowing that their journey would end in a few minutes and that this would be a restful place to sleep, Mary relaxed and enjoyed the last mile of the journey. She arrived in the town eager to find a place to stay, eager to see some old-time friends, and eager to deliver the child that God had placed in her womb.

Questions for Discussion

1. Why did Mary and Joseph go to Bethlehem?
2. What is a census?
3. Why would the journey be so hard?
4. Do you know any psalms Joseph may have sung to Mary?
5. What prophecies are about to be fulfilled now that they are in Bethlehem?
6. Mary and Joseph did something hard to be obedient. Would you be willing to do something difficult to obey God?
7. Did Mary and Joseph find the restful place they had been looking for?

Summary Note

As Mary and Joseph drew closer to Bethlehem, it seemed they drew closer as a couple. Their hearts became one as they looked forward to the fulfillment of prophecy they had heard all of their lives—the Savior would be born in Bethlehem.

DECEMBER 10 | The Bethlehem Inn and the Shepherd's Stable

Luke 2:1-7 | In those days Caesar Augustus issued a decree that a census should be taken of the entire Roman world. (This was the first census that took place while Quirinius was governor of Syria.) And everyone went to their own town to register.

So Joseph also went up from the town of Nazareth in Galilee to Judea, to Bethlehem the town of David, because he belonged to the house and line of David. He went there to register with Mary, who was pledged to be married to him and was expecting a child. While they were there, the time came for the baby to be born, and she gave birth to her firstborn, a son. She wrapped him in cloths and placed him in a manger, because there was no guest room available for them.

After arriving in the city, it no longer seemed a warm and inviting place. The sun had settled over the hills, and darkness filled the air. Mixing with the crowd and trying with little success to find a place to stay made the city seem harsh and uninviting. Joseph took Mary to the inn where he had hoped to spend the night.

After knocking loudly, the door opened to reveal a large room filled with travelers from all parts of the country. Each traveler had been given a tiny section of the floor, just big enough to spread his bed and store his belongings. There was not another foot of floor space left for Mary and Joseph. Seeing the condition of Mary, the innkeeper apologized that he had no private room for her and her husband. He could see that Mary was going to deliver her child very soon. He knew she didn't want to give birth in the public setting of this crowded inn.

However, he did suggest that Mary and Joseph could go outside the city gate to the sheep folds on the edge of town. Here they might find some shepherds who would let them camp in one of their caves. If they were fortunate enough to find one at least she would have a private place in which to give birth to her child.

As Mary and Joseph headed back out of town, perhaps Mary felt the first uneasy cramps of labor begin. She knew that soon she would give birth to the son she had been promised. Hurrying as fast as they dared, they soon arrived at the sheepfolds and found some shepherds who were taking their sheep to the fields. These shepherds, aware of the crowded conditions in Bethlehem, agreed to let them use one of their caves to camp for the evening. Knowing the urgency of Mary's condition, they helped her into the cave and made her comfortable. They then built a fire outside the cave and left Mary alone. Unknowingly, they had just prepared the birthplace of their long expected king. Here, in a cave used as a shelter for sheep, Mary prepared herself and Joseph for the delivery of her firstborn son.

Joseph brought water and a torch and began to comfort Mary as the pain of childbirth became stronger and stronger. He tried to comfort Mary by reminding her of all that had happened in the last nine months. Hearing this, she felt comforted in the fact that she would soon give birth to the son of God. Soon Mary forgot about her surroundings as she concentrated her thoughts and efforts on the birth of their son. She prayed and asked the Lord who had chosen her as a special mother to help her as she delivered this child. As God prepared the heavens and his angels for the announcement of this miraculous birth, Mary struggled to deliver the child—the Christ child, the promised child, the Savior of the world.

Questions for Discussion

1. Was the innkeeper mean because he didn't give Mary and Joseph a place to stay?
2. Is it strange that a king would be born in a stable? Why or why not?
3. Did the shepherds know Mary was going to give birth to Jesus?
4. Would you have given a pregnant lady a place to stay? Why or why not?
5. How did God prepare his angels for this birth?

Summary Note

God provided a private, yet unlikely place, for Mary to have her baby. Here, in a stable used to shelter sheep, she would give birth to Jesus—the Savior of the world, the king.

DECEMBER 11 | The Birth of the Son of God

Luke 2:4-7 | So Joseph also went up from the town of Nazareth in Galilee to Judea, to Bethlehem the town of David, because he belonged to the house and line of David. He went there to register with Mary, who was pledged to be married to him and was expecting a child. While they were there, the time came for the baby to be born, and she gave birth to her firstborn, a son. She wrapped him in cloths and placed him in a manger, because there was no guest room available for them.

Matthew 1:22-23 | All this took place to fulfill what the Lord had said through the prophet: "The virgin will conceive and give birth to a son, and they will call him Immanuel" (which means "God with us").

Throughout the long night Mary had struggled with the pain of childbirth. Suddenly, the time of birth came, and Jesus was pushed from her womb. Joseph, helping all he could, heard a loud cry fill the stable. Tears clouded his eyes as he took the child and cradled him to his chest. Mary, now exhausted, lay weeping as she stroked her firstborn son. Joseph handed him back to her, and she felt the warmth of his tiny body against hers. The long expected moment had arrived at last. She now held in her arms the promised child. She was holding God. This tiny baby was the Great I Am. Sensing the chill that filled the stable, Mary asked Joseph to get the clothes they had brought for the child. Joseph unwrapped the small bundle and handed them to Mary. She slowly dressed the child and thanked God that he was such a perfect baby.

Then, content that the baby was well covered and warm, she began to feed him. As she fed him, she softly talked to him about who he was and what he was going to do. She told him where they were and about his ancestor David who had walked these very hills. Joseph, with his strong and powerful hands, lovingly prepared a bed in the manger which was just the right size to hold a baby. After the feeding was over, Joseph took the child and laid him in the manger, gently covering him with the hay. He also thanked God for such a beautiful child.

After the baby settled and fell asleep, Joseph returned to Mary. Holding hands, they began to cry as they thought about the miraculous way in which their son had been born. They began to share the marvel of what had happened and why it had happened. They smiled with joy when they thought of Isaiah's prophecy knowing that Mary was the promised virgin, and the baby was the promised son. Finally, they sat in deep silence holding each other as they thought of the child's name—Immanuel, God with us.

Silently, contentedly, safe in each other arms and in the watch care of God, Mary and Joseph worshipped their heavenly father. They realized he had now brought to his people a Savior, a deliverer—as he has promised Abraham so many years ago. These first witnesses of the birth of Christ wondered what life with this child would be like.

Questions for Discussion

1. How did Mary feel about having a baby in a stable?
2. Why did God want Christ to be born in a stable?
3. What do you think Mary and Joseph talked about after the baby was born?
4. How was this birth a fulfillment of prophecy?
5. Would you have liked to have been there? Why or why not?

Summary Note

Mary gave birth to her son in an out of the way, lowly place—a stable. However, that place would soon become a place of holy worship as the shepherds came back to their stable to see their promised king.

DECEMBER 12 | The Angel of the Lord and an Angelic Choir

Luke 2:8-14 | And there were shepherds living out in the fields nearby, keeping watch over their flocks at night. An angel of the Lord appeared to them, and the glory of the Lord shone around them, and they were terrified. But the angel said to them, "Do not be afraid. I bring you good news that will cause great joy for all the people. Today in the town of David a Savior has been born to you; he is the Messiah, the Lord. This will be a sign to you: You will find a baby wrapped in cloths and lying in a manger."

Suddenly a great company of the heavenly host appeared with the angel, praising God and saying,

"Glory to God in the highest heaven,

and on earth peace to those on whom his favor rests."

As Mary and Joseph worshipped together and praised God for their newborn son, God was preparing the heavens for the announcement of this long awaited birth. The angel of the Lord was once again called into God's presence and given another assignment. He was to appear to the band of shepherds who had loaned their stable to Mary and Joseph and give them a special message.

As the angel of the Lord made his way to the shepherds' fields, the glory of the Lord went with him. Heaven and earth seemed to meet as he stood before the dazzled eyes of the shepherds. The glory of the Lord which followed him lit up the whole plain as it settled over the group and surrounded them in a mantle of heavenly light. Surprise, fear, and awe struck the shepherds.

The angel softly spoke and told them not to be afraid. He told them that he had a message of great joy—a message that would cause them and others to rejoice. "Today," he said, "in the town of Bethlehem, a Savior has been born to you; he is Christ the Lord." This message was recognized by the shepherds as the promise of the long awaited Savior. They thought of what they had been taught for many years in the temple—that the Savior would be born in Bethlehem, just as the prophet Micah had prophesied (see day 1). The angel gave them a sign so they would recognize the child—"You will find the baby wrapped in clothes and lying in a manger."

This statement was a signal for the other heaven sent angels to burst upon the scene. They broke through the heavens with a song on their lips. It was a song of worship and praise. It was a song of worship to the son of God. The first part of this song was a verse of worship to God. They glorified God for sending his son to this earth. The second part stated the result of the coming of the Savior—peace on earth to men. As the angelic choir raised this hymn of praise, the shepherds began to comprehend and understand the message they were receiving.

Then as suddenly as they had appeared, the hymn ceased, the light faded, the angels ascended to heaven, and the shepherds were left alone. The angels had completed their task and now returned to the heavens to await their next mission and to observe what happened with the child and the shepherds.

Questions for Discussion

1. What was the "glory of the Lord?"
2. Why were the shepherds afraid?
3. What was the angel's message?
4. What sign did the angel give them?
5. How many angels were in the choir? (According to Hebrews 1:6, all of them.)
6. What does "glory to God in the highest" mean?
7. Would you have been afraid? Why or why not?
8. If you were a shepherd, what would you do now?
9. What do you do when you read a command in God's word?

Summary Note

The angel of the Lord came to announce the advent of the Savior to a group of shepherds. He was joined by an angelic choir that praised God for sending his son to this earth. When the angels went away, this special appearance caused the shepherds to run and find the Christ child so that they too could worship him.

Luke 2:15-20 | When the angels had left them and gone into heaven, the shepherds said to one another, "Let's go to Bethlehem and see this thing that has happened, which the Lord has told us about."

So they hurried off and found Mary and Joseph, and the baby, who was lying in the manger. When they had seen him, they spread the word concerning what had been told them about this child, and all who heard it were amazed at what the shepherds said to them. But Mary treasured up all these things and pondered them in her heart. The shepherds returned, glorifying and praising God for all the things they had heard and seen, which were just as they had been told.

The angelic message had stopped, and the glory of the Lord had faded from the plain. Darkness, still and cold, once again settled on the land. Each shepherd, alone with his thoughts, sat down in silence. The only sound was the bleating of the sheep.

After sitting for several minutes in silence and unbelief, the shepherds began to talk about the events which had happened. The message they had been told began to stir their souls and direct them back to the cave which they had earlier prepared for a young expectant mother. Finally, with much excitement and expectation, they decided to follow the angelic message and go and find the baby.

Leaving one young boy and their dogs to guard the sheep, they hurriedly left for the cave. Along the way they began to ask each other some questions. Will we find a baby, wrapped in cloths, lying in our manger? How can we know that what we were told is the truth? Was it all a dream? What will we do when we find him?

In a few minutes they arrived at the cave. Out of breath, they paused outside and praised God that they were about to meet the promised Savior. Slowly and quietly they crept into the cave and across the rustling straw. Then they knelt and gazed at the baby. Partly they worshipped the newborn king, and partly they wondered at all that had happened in the last hour. Directed by the Holy Spirit, each shepherd worshipped the tiny king and thanked God that he had sent this promised Savior. By faith they had believed the message of the angel, and now this faith was made sight—they saw and worshipped the Savior.

Quietly the shepherds told Mary and Joseph of the angelic visit. They told them of their fear, of the

angel's calm assurance, and of the message the angel •
gave to them. They described the lighting of the plain
by the glory of the Lord and the song of the angelic
choir. They told of their own excitement as they ran to
see the promised, yet newborn, king.

Mary and Joseph, by now as excited as the
shepherds, shared their own stories of an angelic visit,
of their fear, of the angel's calm assurance, and of the
message the angel had spoken. The three messages fit
together so well and told such a beautiful story. It was
a story that could not be kept a secret. The shepherds
ran from the stable and told this wonderful story to all
they met. They told how on this night a prophecy
hundreds of years old had been fulfilled (Micah 5:2).
Perhaps they knocked on every door in Bethlehem.
Perhaps they went to the very inn where there had
been no room for Mary and Joseph. Excited beyond
belief, they told everyone—in the stables, in the fields,
in the town, and perhaps later in the temple—of the
wonderful message they had been told and of the
Savior they had seen. Those who heard the message
were amazed and must have retold the story on their
way home and to all their relatives at home. All of
Bethlehem reacted, but none as Mary did. She
treasured these events and thought about them in her
heart. She replayed each event in her mind, and she

pictured the fulfillment of God's promises which had been given to her nine months before.

As the night gave way to the first light of dawn, peace returned to the cave and Mary rested. The shepherds, with love in their hearts and praise on their lips, returned to their flocks. Perhaps on this very night the wise men began their long journey which would bring them to this newborn king.

Questions for Discussion

1. What did the shepherds do after the angels left?

2. What would you have done if you were one of the shepherds?

3. How were the angelic visits to Mary, Joseph, and the shepherds alike?

4. If you were a shepherd what questions would you have liked to ask Mary after you saw the baby?

5. How would you worship a newborn king? What would you say or sing?

6. Would you be willing to spread the news about this newborn king to your town? What would you say to your friends and neighbors?

Summary Note

The story of the birth of this special baby was spread throughout Bethlehem and the surrounding region during the next several days. People from all walks of life heard it and repeated it. Shepherds, merchants, travelers, weavers, farmers, priests, and many others spread the story as they went about their daily lives. Perhaps Simeon and Anna, two great servants of God at the temple, heard the message and waited expectantly for the appearance of this newborn king.

DECEMBER 14 | Presentation in the Temple

Luke 2:21-24 | On the eighth day, when it was time to circumcise the child, he was named Jesus, the name the angel had given him before he was conceived.

When the time came for the purification rites required by the Law of Moses, Joseph and Mary took him to Jerusalem to present him to the Lord (as it is written in the Law of the Lord, "Every firstborn male is to be consecrated to the Lord"), and to offer a sacrifice in keeping with what is said in the Law of the Lord: "a pair of doves or two young pigeons."

Eight days after Jesus was born Joseph and Mary called together a few friends and family members so they could be witnesses to the circumcision of their firstborn son. This circumcision ceremony would be done in obedience to the Law of Moses. This law required that when the baby was eight days old he should be circumcised and given a name. This ceremony was a sign that the baby belonged to God and that as he grew he would worship and obey God. It also showed that the baby was a member of the Jewish race and could claim the promises God had made to that nation.

At this ceremony the parents were to name the baby. Surely Joseph remembered back to that night when the angel had first appeared to him and told him that Mary was going to have a baby. The angel had given him a heaven-sent name for the child. He repeated the name out loud and thought about its meaning. He recalled how the angel had said that the baby born to Mary would be the Savior of his people. His eyes filled with tears as he told his gathered friends and family that the child's name would be Jesus. Perhaps he repeated once again the story of this miraculous birth. After their friends and family had gone home, he and Mary may once again have talked of God's faithfulness, goodness, and love. They talked of how Jesus would grow and when he was a man how he would be the Savior of his people.

It was also a law among the Jews that forty days after the first child was born in a family that he would be brought to the temple and presented to the priest. Here a burnt offering would be made for him to the Lord. This offering of a lamb or a dove showed that he belonged to the Lord. It also was an expression of his parents' love and worship to God. They were expressing thankfulness for what God had done through them. After the burnt offering was sacrificed, Mary would make her way to another part of the temple where she would offer up a sin offering to the Lord. For this offering a lamb or a dove was sacrificed as a payment for sin. The sacrifice of this dove would be the payment for Mary's sin.

And so, forty days after Jesus' birth, Joseph and Mary made the five and a half mile trip to Jerusalem for the purpose of sacrificing the burnt offering and the sin offering. Since they were poor and could not afford a lamb, they took along two young doves to be used as sacrifices. Jesus was presented to the priest, and a dove was offered up as a burnt offering. Then Mary presented herself to the priest, told of her days of purification, and offered a dove as her sin offering. As she did this, did she think about her son and how the angel had said he would be the Savior of his people? Did she understand that her son would grow up and become the one sacrifice that could take away the sin of the world? Perhaps she thought of this as she laid her hand on the head of the dove as a symbol of transferring her sin to the dove. Knowing that the dove would be killed and his blood shed as a symbol of redemption for sin, did she think about the destiny of her son? Soon some of these questions would be answered as a Spirit-filled old man named Simeon would see the baby and prophecy about his life.

Questions for Discussion

1. Why did Joseph and Mary obey the Law of Moses?
2. What is circumcision? (Your child will probably ask this.)
3. What does the name Jesus mean?
4. Why did they bring doves to be their sacrifice?
5. Who has paid for our sin?
6. Do you believe that Jesus died to pay for your sin?

Summary Note

Mary and Joseph had done everything required by the Law of Moses. They had made the offerings in obedience to the commands of the Lord. As they prepared to return to Bethlehem, they were met by two godly people who told them some marvelous things about their newborn son.

DECEMBER 15 | Prophecy of Simeon

Luke 2:25-35 | Now there was a man in Jerusalem called Simeon, who was righteous and devout. He was waiting for the consolation of Israel, and the Holy Spirit was on him. It had been revealed to him by the Holy Spirit that he would not die before he had seen the Lord's Messiah. Moved by the Spirit, he went into the temple courts. When the parents brought in the child Jesus to do for him what the custom of the Law required, Simeon took him in his arms and praised God, saying:

> "Sovereign Lord, as you have promised,
> you may now dismiss your servant in peace.
> For my eyes have seen your salvation,
> which you have prepared in the sight of all nations:
> a light for revelation to the Gentiles,
> and the glory of your people Israel."

The child's father and mother marveled at what was said about him. Then Simeon blessed them and said to Mary, his mother: "This child is destined to cause the falling and rising of many in Israel, and to be a sign that will be spoken against, so that the thoughts of many hearts will be revealed. And a sword will pierce your own soul too."

As Mary and Joseph came into the courtyard looking for a priest to officiate for them at the altar, they were met by an old man name Simeon. Old Simeon was a very religious man who had been waiting for the Christ to come and deliver the Jewish nation from their sin and their political enemies.

Simeon, who may have been a priest, was very well known to the people who came to the temple. He had been there for many, many years. He was known as one who always obeyed the commandments of the Lord. He came to the temple often to worship his God. He was a very devout man. Simeon had a very interesting story that he would share with those who gathered in the temple courtyard. He would tell his friends and the other worshippers how he had lived righteously all of his life. He would tell them of the excitement he felt when he read the Old Testament prophecies that told of the coming of the Lord's Christ. He told them how he prayed that these prophecies would be fulfilled in his lifetime. Finally, he would tell them that one morning while he was praying the Holy Spirit told him that he would not die until he saw the one who would be the Savior of his people. This was a message that gave him great hope as he came each day to worship in the temple.

This very morning the Holy Spirit had come to Simeon and told him he must go to the temple. Sensing that something special was going to happen, he hurried to dress and went quickly to the temple. As he arrived at the courtyard, the Holy Spirit directed him to a young couple with a baby. They were crossing the courtyard looking for a priest. Suddenly it shot through him like a flash of lightening that this was the one whom he had waited so long to see. He knew that this little one was the promised Christ. Overjoyed by this message, Simeon rushed to the young couple and asked to hold the baby.

Holding the baby toward heaven, Simeon began to prophecy in the name of the Lord. He began by saying that the promise God had given him had been kept. God had permitted him to see the Savior, and now he was ready to die. But the prophecy didn't stop with this statement. He also prophesied three things about the child:

1. This child was the one who would bring salvation to all people. (The apostle John told of the fulfillment of this prophecy when he said that Jesus would take away the sins of the world; see John 1:29-34.)

2. This child would be a light, and he would give light to many nations. (Jesus confirmed this prophecy

when he told his followers that he was the light of the world; see John 8:12.)

3. This child would be the glory of the Jewish nation. (This prophecy was also given by Isaiah when he prophesied of the deliverance of Israel; see Isaiah 60:19).

When Mary and Joseph heard these prophecies, they were amazed. Simeon gave them a blessing in the name of the Lord. Their hearts were overflowing with joy and excitement. Finally, Simeon had a solemn message for Mary. He told her that the baby would cause many in Israel to fall and to rise again. He also told her that many would speak against her son and in the end sorrow would pierce her soul. Before he could explain this message, another servant of God joined the group. Her name was Anna. She told of the redemption that this child would bring.

Questions for Discussion

1. Why did God tell Simeon he would not die until he saw Jesus?
2. What does it mean that Jesus would bring salvation to all people?
3. What does it mean that Jesus would be a light?
4. Do you know any other Old Testament prophecies about Christ?
5. What did Simeon mean when he said that a sword would pierce Mary's soul?
6. Who do you know that is like Simeon: they love God, they obey his commandments, and they worship him?

Summary Note

Once again Mary and Joseph were amazed by the message they had just heard. Perhaps they remembered that they had heard these same prophecies when their priest had read the book of Isaiah in their synagogue (see Isaiah 60). But, the message did not end here. Once again another servant of God spoke to them and gave them a heaven-sent message about their newborn son.

DECEMBER 16 | Prophecy of Anna

Luke 2:36-40 | There was also a prophet, Anna, the daughter of Penuel, of the tribe of Asher. She was very old; she had lived with her husband seven years after her marriage, and then was a widow until she was eighty-four. She never left the temple but worshiped night and day, fasting and praying. Coming up to them at that very moment, she gave thanks to God and spoke about the child to all who were looking forward to the redemption of Jerusalem.

When Joseph and Mary had done everything required by the Law of the Lord, they returned to Galilee to their own town of Nazareth. And the child grew and became strong; he was filled with wisdom, and the grace of God was on him.

A small crowd began to gather around Simeon after he took the baby. The crowd listened to his prophecy and rejoiced with him as he told how the child would be a light and would be the glory of Israel. They listened intently and wondered what he meant when he told Mary her soul would be pierced. Just as he completed this solemn message to Mary, a woman in the crowd began to prophecy about the child. She spoke about the redemption the child would bring. The crowd turned to see who was speaking, and they recognized Anna. She, like Simeon, had been waiting many, many years to see the one who would be the Savior of Israel. The crowd listened with great interest to her message, because they knew she was a very godly woman. She had been ministering in the temple for many years. Her worship and service to God was known by all who came to the temple area. Anna had married at an early age, perhaps fourteen or fifteen. After being married only seven years, her husband died. She chose not to remarry but to serve God at the temple. She was now eighty-four, and she lived in the temple area.

Anna's life was one of worship, prayer, and fasting. Because she lived such a devoted life, God had made her a prophetess, and she ministered to many people as they came to worship at the temple. Now God gave her his greatest prophecy—this child would be the redeemer of Israel. Knowing about her life of devotion and service to God, the crowd believed what she said about the baby. They had heard a wonderful message—this child would be the redeemer. They didn't realize that this prophecy fit so well with the solemn prophecy of Simeon. The way that this child would bring redemption would be the very thing that would pierce his mother's soul. He would lay down his life as a sacrifice for the sins of the world. Surely this death, even though it would bring redemption to his people, would send a piercing sword through his mother's soul. These two prophecies, given by two different servants of God, looked forward to the reason Christ came to this earth. He came to be the sacrifice for sin, and dying was the only way he could redeem his people.

Anna, though not understanding the full impact of her prophecy, thanked God that she had seen the child. She praised God that the promised redeemer had come to earth.

Questions for Discussion

1. What is a prophetess?
2. What does fasting mean?
3. Why did God choose to give this message to Anna?
4. What is a redeemer?
5. How would Christ be a redeemer?
6. Christ died for the sins of the world. Have you asked him to forgive you for your sins?

Summary Note

In a few minutes the crowd went away, and Mary and Joseph went to find the priest. Simeon and Anna once again shared their joy at seeing the promised Christ. They prayed together and worshipped the God whose promise they had believed for so many years. As they prayed, in a distant country other worshippers set out to find this promised Christ. These travelers had seen a star in the east and were now on their way to find this newborn king.

DECEMBER 17 | Wise Men Worship the King

Matthew 2:1-12 | After Jesus was born in Bethlehem in Judea, during the time of King Herod, Magi from the east came to Jerusalem and asked, "Where is the one who has been born king of the Jews? We saw his star when it rose and have come to worship him."

When King Herod heard this he was disturbed, and all Jerusalem with him. When he had called together all the people's chief priests and teachers of the law, he asked them where the Messiah was to be born. "In Bethlehem in Judea," they replied, "for this is what the prophet has written:

"'But you, Bethlehem, in the land of Judah,
are by no means least among the rulers of Judah;
for out of you will come a ruler
who will shepherd my people Israel.'"

Then Herod called the Magi secretly and found out from them the exact time the star had appeared. He sent them to Bethlehem and said, "Go and search carefully for the child. As soon as you find him, report to me so that I too may go and worship him."

After they had heard the king, they went on their way, and the star they had seen when it rose went ahead of them until it stopped over the place where the child was. When they saw the star, they were overjoyed. On coming to the house, they saw the child with his mother Mary, and they bowed down and worshiped him. Then they opened their treasures and presented him with gifts of gold, frankincense and myrrh. And having been warned in a dream not to go back to Herod, they returned to their country by another route.

Several months after the prophecies of Simeon and Anna, certain wise men from the east arrived in Jerusalem with some startling news and some strange questions. These priest-sages had seen a star in a country to the east of their homeland. They believed the star announced the birth of a child who would be the king of the Jews. They wanted to come and pay homage to him. After traveling possibly a thousand miles, they came to the capital city, Jerusalem, believing they would find him there.

The arrival of the wise men was an unforgettable event. The size of their caravan, the number of servants, and the riches they displayed amazed all who saw them. However, their questions to the people were even more amazing. They wanted to know where they could find the newborn king. They stated that they had come to worship him. These questions and the fact that they wanted to worship a newborn king disturbed the inhabitants of the city. Even King Herod was upset. In his fright at this news, Herod called for the help of the Jewish priests. He asked them where a king was to be born. The answer was easy. They simply quoted him Micah 5:2 which said that the Christ would be born in Bethlehem. Herod, anxious to find the child and kill him, called in the wise men and asked them when the star had appeared. After they answered his question, he asked them to inform him of the whereabouts of the child. He told the wise men that he would join them as they worshipped the child.

As the wise men left the king, the star they had seen several months earlier reappeared and led them to a house in the city of Bethlehem. The wise men began to rejoice as they saw the house and knew that their long search was over. With excitement they dismounted from their camels, uncovered their gifts, straightened their robes and turbans, and stepped toward the entrance of the house.

When the wise men were taken into the room where the young child was, they promptly fell on the ground and worshipped him. This bowing down showed that they were bowing their hearts to him.

Seeing the child, this promised Savior, they adored him with all of their being. Next they presented him with gifts of gold, frankincense, and myrrh. These were indeed gifts fit for a king. They could be used for worship, perfume, medicine, and even embalming. They were the best the wise men had. Finally, after several months of searching, they had met the Christ and fulfilled the desire of their hearts. They had worshipped him by giving of themselves and by giving of the best they had.

Questions for Discussion

1. Why was Herod so upset by the announcement of the birth of a new king?
2. Why did the wise men come?
3. How do you think the wise men felt when they arrived at the house?
4. What gift would you give a newborn king?
5. How can we worship Christ?
6. Are you willing to give Christ your best—your life and the best things that you have?

Summary Note

After talking with Mary and Joseph, the wise men possibly went to the Bethlehem inn to spend the night. But their night's sleep was not to be very long. During the night God told them in a dream of Herod's true intent for the Christ. Immediately they got up and had the animals loaded. The whole caravan started back to their homeland. Little did they know how this departure would trigger the anger of the suspicious and outraged king.

DECEMBER 18 | Joseph's Second Dream

Matthew 2:13-14 | When they had gone, an angel of the Lord appeared to Joseph in a dream. "Get up," he said, "take the child and his mother and escape to Egypt. Stay there until I tell you, for Herod is going to search for the child to kill him."

So he got up, took the child and his mother during the night and left for Egypt.

As the caravan of the wise men was leaving the city of Bethlehem, God in heaven once again summoned his angel and sent him to Joseph. Joseph had gone to bed a peaceful man. His child was well; the wise men had visited, worshipped the child, and given him expensive gifts. As Joseph and Mary went to bed, they probably spoke again of the wonderful ways God was working in their lives and in the life of their son. All that was happening was confirming the messages he and Mary had been given about the holy child.

In the middle of the night Joseph's rest was disturbed by the angel of the Lord appearing to him. This time there was no fear. Joseph recognized the angel and was eager to hear his message. The angel told him to take the child and his mother and escape to Egypt. "Escape to Egypt?" Joseph thought. "Why? There is no danger here." Then the angel told Joseph why he must go to Egypt. Herod wanted to kill the child. It was an unbelievable message. Cruel Herod wanted to kill an innocent child! Cruel Herod wanted to kill the one who was born to be the Savior! Cruel Herod wanted to kill the child who he thought would take his throne!

Joseph could hardly believe what he was hearing. But, knowing that this was a warning from heaven and that the child truly was in danger, Joseph did what he had been instructed to do. He arose immediately, dressed, and woke Mary. Together they packed only the items they would need. Remembering the gifts of the wise men, they hid them in their belongings. Joseph knew that embalmers of Egypt would pay a high price for the myrrh. This myrrh and the other gifts could be sold for a large sum of money which could then support the family for several months. Silently, Joseph again thanked God for the visit of the wise men and their gifts. These gifts would now support a family that was being driven from Bethlehem by a king who was mad.

After Joseph and Mary had prepared their belongings, they wrapped the child and slipped quietly out of town before dawn. When the sun rose the next morning, they were well on their way to Beersheba and then on south to the land of Egypt. They traveled at a quick pace. They were eager to get out of the country and away from the power of Herod. As they traveled, they continually prayed that God would save the child from the fury and wrath of the wicked king.

Questions for Discussion

1. Why wasn't Joseph afraid of the angel this time?
2. Was the message hard to believe? Why or why not?
3. Could Joseph have done something else, something easier? Why did he obey the angel?
4. Why would a king want to kill a baby?
5. What do you think the trip to Egypt was like?
6. Joseph and Mary were obedient even though they had to do a hard thing. Are you willing to be obedient to God even if it is hard?

Summary Note

God's timing is always perfect. He sent the wise men to worship the newborn king and give him expensive gifts. Now these gifts would be used to support Joseph's family while they were hiding in Egypt. Hopefully, these gifts or the money from them could be used for the return trip to their homeland.

DECEMBER 19 | Journey to Egypt

Matthew 2:13-15a | When they had gone, an angel of the Lord appeared to Joseph in a dream. "Get up," he said, "take the child and his mother and escape to Egypt. Stay there until I tell you, for Herod is going to search for the child to kill him."

So he got up, took the child and his mother during the night and left for Egypt, where he stayed until the death of Herod.

Hastily Joseph and Mary had prepared for this trip. Now, hours later and still on the road, they were hungry and tired. At noon they stopped to eat and rest the donkey. After eating, Mary fed the child, and they began to discuss the journey. Joseph believed it might take them three days of hard travel to reach the border of Egypt which was seventy-five miles away. Once there they could relax and travel at a slower pace, because they would be in a land where Herod had no power. Joseph also thought it might take them another five or six days to reach a Jewish city where they might find a place to live. Here, about one hundred miles inside the country, he could look for a job so he could support this family.

Deciding they had better talk about other details of the trip as they walked, they loaded the donkey and again headed south. At least for Mary traveling was a little easier this time. She was not pregnant, and she had recovered well from the birth of her child. She worried though about the effects of the trip on the child. They were traveling through the desert, and there was the danger that they were being pursued by Herod's men.

However, for Joseph this trip was especially hard. He was running to a foreign country knowing that a king wanted to find him and kill Mary's son. Joseph was very careful about who he talked to and about what he said. Each night was a restless night as he was afraid that Herod's soldiers could appear and take away the child. It seemed that the only way he could go to sleep was to pray himself to sleep. As he prayed, it seemed God filled him with a peaceful spirit as he reminded Joseph how he had always kept his word.

About three days after leaving Bethlehem Joseph and Mary arrived at the border. Joseph probably had sold some of the frankincense and bought supplies for the next several days. After resting for a short while, they traveled on until nightfall and found a place to stop for the night. As they settled down and prayed again for God's protection, perhaps they talked about all that God had done in their lives during the last eighteen to twenty-four months. They were amazed at how God was continuing to work in their lives and how he was protecting the baby. One question that was sure to cross their minds was this— why was this happening? It was not a question of anger toward God but a question for which they didn't even expect an answer. They knew that each event in the life of their son was a special, planned event. They may have asked each other what the reason was for this trip into Egypt and why this mad king wanted to kill their child.

Finally, after several days of travel, Joseph and Mary arrived at a Jewish community. Here they found a place to live, and Joseph began to look for a job. Did they tell the people about their son and his special birth? Or did they quietly settle into the community and wait for the promised message from God? At least while they were here they were safe from the hatred of Herod. Jesus had a safe and quiet place in which he could begin to grow up.

Questions for Discussion

1.   What supplies do you think they took?
2.   What do you think Joseph asked for each night when he prayed?
3.   They may have asked why this was happening. Why was it happening?
4.   Joseph was obedient again. This shows he was a godly man. Are you obedient to God and his word? Are you a godly person?
5.   Does God direct our lives just as he directed Joseph and Mary's lives?

Summary Note

Joseph probably found a job as a carpenter, and he and Mary settled into the community. Possibly they discussed how God had used two rulers in their lives. One ruler had declared a tax, forcing them to travel to Bethlehem. Here, in fulfillment of prophecy, their son had been born. Another ruler had wanted to kill their son, forcing them to flee to Egypt. This too was a fulfillment of prophecy.

DECEMBER 20 | Herod the King

Matthew 2:7-8 | Then Herod called the Magi secretly and found out from them the exact time the star had appeared. He sent them to Bethlehem and said, "Go and search carefully for the child. As soon as you find him, report to me, so that I too may go and worship him."

Matthew 2:16-18 | When Herod realized that he had been outwitted by the Magi, he was furious, and he gave orders to kill all the boys in Bethlehem and its vicinity who were two years old and under, in accordance with the time he had learned from the Magi. Then what was said through the prophet Jeremiah was fulfilled:

> "A voice is heard in Ramah,
> weeping and great mourning,
> Rachel weeping for her children
> and refusing to be comforted,
> because they are no more."

A most upsetting event had occurred in the city of Jerusalem. Wise men had come in search of a newborn king. They had been permitted to see King Herod, and they had questioned him about a new son.

King Herod, to whom no son had just been born, became fearful that this newborn king would one day rise up and take his throne. He determined in his heart that he would find the king and kill him. Would a king really do this? Would a grown man really kill an innocent baby? This king would! When he feared that his sons might take his throne, he had them killed. When he began to distrust his wife, he had her killed. He was a king whose reign was marked by bloodshed. Anyone who opposed him would be put to death. It didn't matter who they were—family, friend, or enemy.

After the visit of the wise men, Herod called the scribes so that he could find out where the baby was to be born. Having learned that he would be born in Bethlehem, he wanted to find out when he had been born. Pretending that he wanted to worship the newborn king, he called the wise men back into his palace and asked them when they had seen the star. Then, with his blessing, he sent them to Bethlehem to find the child. He requested that they return to his palace after finding the child so that he could join them in worshipping this king.

Herod was truly a deceptive and evil man. As he waited for the wise men to return and tell him where he could find the child, he secretly plotted as to how he could get rid of this newborn king. However, God knew what Herod was thinking. He told the wise men in a dream not to return to Herod but to go home by another route. They quickly and quietly did as they were told.

After waiting several days for the wise men to return, Herod realized that they had somehow discovered his plot to kill the child. When he learned that they had left his country, his anger burst forth like a storm. He was furious. Realizing that he did not know which child in Bethlehem was the newborn king, he decided to kill all the boys who had been born in the last two years. By having his soldiers kill all of them, he believed they would kill the Christ child. Herod called his soldiers and gave them their orders. They mounted their horses and rode swiftly to Bethlehem. All of Bethlehem was frightened as they rode into town with their swords raised. No one knew why they were there or what they were looking for until they found a two-year old child and killed him. Like madmen they searched the town and without mercy killed every male child under the age of two. They would break into homes, find the child, and kill him right in front of his family.

The townspeople were in shock. Many were screaming and crying. Others were trying to drive the soldiers away. Others were trying to find hiding places for their young sons. But there were too many soldiers, and they were well armed. Finally, knowing they had killed every young boy, the soldiers rode out of town and disappeared over the hills toward Jerusalem. All that was heard in Bethlehem was the crying of mothers as they held their dead babies in their arms. Surely anger and grief filled their hearts. These senseless killings caused the whole region to grieve. This too was a fulfillment of prophecy. The prophet Jeremiah had said that in this region the mothers would weep loudly because their sons had been killed (see Jeremiah 31:15).

God had worked in a strange way. The Savior was safe in another country, but several other innocent babies had been killed. Herod, in his madness, had actually driven Joseph and Mary out of his country into Egypt. This action would make it possible for another prophecy to be fulfilled. The prophet Hosea had said that God would call his son out of Egypt (see Hosea 11:1). Herod had driven the child there, and God would call him out when Herod was dead.

Questions for Discussion

1. Why was Herod so upset when he heard a king was born?
2. Why was Herod such a cruel king?
3. Why wouldn't Herod tell the wise men that he wanted to kill the newborn king?
4. How would you feel if your baby brother was killed by some soldiers?
5. Would you try to stop the soldiers? How?

Summary Note

This story would be so different if Herod had really joined the wise men and gone to worship the Christ child. He would have shown that he was also a very wise man. Instead, Herod is remembered for his cruelty and madness. The sweetest words heard in that country since the announcement of Christ's birth were these: Herod is dead! The announcement of his death was a signal for the return of the Christ child to the land of his birth.

Matthew 2:19-21, 15b, 22-23 | After Herod died, an angel of the Lord appeared in a dream to Joseph in Egypt and said, "Get up, take the child and his mother and go to the land of Israel, for those who were trying to take the child's life are dead."

So he got up, took the child and his mother and went to the land of Israel.

And so was fulfilled what the Lord had said through the prophet: "Out of Egypt I called my son."

But when he heard that Archelaus was reigning in Judea in place of his father Herod, he was afraid to go there. Having been warned in a dream, he withdrew to the district of Galilee, and he went and lived in a town called Nazareth. So was fulfilled what was said through the prophets, that he would be called a Nazarene.

To the people who lived in the land of Israel there could have been no better news. Herod was dead, and the inhabitants of the land rejoiced. But this joy was short-lived as Archelaus, the son of Herod, became king. He too was a cruel leader. His crimes against his people were so bad that the Emperor took away his power and authority and exiled him from the country. He was no longer the king. In fact, Pontius Pilate was made the Roman governor of Judea.

Joseph also had good reason to rejoice. One evening after he had gone to bed the angel of the Lord appeared to him again. Joseph welcomed this appearance and learned some wonderful news. Herod was dead, and it was time to take the child and return to their homeland. Not able to wait until morning, perhaps he woke Mary and told her the wonderful news. The next day was filled with excitement as they told their new friends, packed their belongings, and prepared for the long trip home. Possibly they decided to spend one last night in Egypt so that they would be well rested for the journey.

The first few days of the trip seemed easy as they made their way to the border of Israel. They talked about their family and friends whom they had not seen for perhaps several years. They thought of many of the things that had occurred in the last three years, and their hearts were filled with joy. Each night when they rested they thanked God that they were able to return to their homeland.

As they traveled, this family was fulfilling another prophecy about the Savior. The prophet Hosea had said that God would call his son out of

Egypt, and this was exactly what was happening. The son of God was indeed being called out of Egypt. He was going home to the land of his forefathers.

After crossing from Egypt into Israel, Joseph began to talk to some travelers. They told him the good news of Herod's death. However, they also told him that Archelaus was now king and that his crimes were much worse than those of his father. Joseph began to worry about going to Bethlehem and being so close to the capital where this evil king reigned. He and Mary talked about what they should do. The excitement of the trip now faded as they faced the possibility of having to hide again. Where would they run to? Should they return to Egypt? Would this king try to kill Jesus? These questions may have troubled their minds as they went to bed that night. Now instead of peaceful sleep they again were restless as they thought about Archelaus and what could happen. They prayed that God would protect their child. God, knowing their distress, decided to send the angel one last time with a message of hope. And so, as Joseph slept, the angel appeared again. This time Joseph was relieved when he saw him. He knew that God had sent the angel to tell him what he and Mary should do. The message was simple: go to Galilee and live there. The child will be safe there. Joseph did as he had always done before—he immediately obeyed.

Joseph woke Mary and told her of the angelic appearance. When it was light enough to travel, they started for the region of Galilee. This was the region from which they had begun their journey so long ago. Nazareth, their hometown, was in Galilee. They hurried as fast as they could the last two days of the journey. Once again they would see family and friends they had not seen in a long time. The excitement of this reunion filled them as they approached the city. Perhaps they discussed how the angel had first appeared here and given them the unbelievable messages about their son. Again, their arrival at Nazareth was a fulfillment of prophecy, that Jesus would be called a Nazarene.

Questions for Discussion

1. Two prophecies were fulfilled in this part of the story. Do you remember some others that we have read about?
2. Do you know any prophecies that tell about Jesus when he becomes a man?
3. Do you think Archelaus would have tried to kill Jesus? Why or why not?
4. How do you think Joseph and Mary felt when they knew they were going to live in Nazareth?
5. What do you think they told their parents and friends when they arrived in the city?

Summary Note

Mary and Joseph had finally returned to the city of Nazareth. Special memories unfolded as they thought about the angelic appearances that had announced they would be the parents of the Christ child. They thought of the long journey they had taken. They discussed how God had always protected them. Now they had brought their child home. It was here he would grow up and become a strong young man. This was the place from which he would begin a life of service and ministry to others.

DECEMBER 22 | Nazareth and His Childhood

Luke 2:41-52 | Every year Jesus' parents went to Jerusalem for the Festival of the Passover. When he was twelve years old, they went up to the festival, according to the custom. After the festival was over, while his parents were returning home, the boy Jesus stayed behind in Jerusalem, but they were unaware of it. Thinking he was in their company, they traveled on for a day. Then they began looking for him among their relatives and friends. When they did not find him, they went back to Jerusalem to look for him. After three days they found him in the temple courts, sitting among the teachers, listening to them and asking them questions. Everyone who heard him was amazed at his understanding and his answers. When his parents saw him, they were astonished. His mother said to him, "Son, why have you treated us like this? Your father and I have been anxiously searching for you."

"Why were you searching for me?" he asked. "Didn't you know I had to be in my Father's house?" But they did not understand what he was saying to them.

Then he went down to Nazareth with them and was obedient to them. But his mother treasured all these things in her heart. And Jesus grew in wisdom and stature, and in favor with God and man.

God had called Joseph and his family out of Egypt, and they had settled in Nazareth. Jesus was to live in this city until he was thirty years old. We know little about his boyhood, youth, or young manhood. It is very likely that he lived in a one-room house with a dirt floor. During the day Jesus would sit on a cushion on the floor, and at night he probably slept on a mat which was rolled up and put away in the morning. His life was that of a common person in a small country town. It was a very humble upbringing for such a special child.

Jesus may have been educated at home by his mother or at a village school which was held in the synagogue. He was taught to read and write. His lessons were from the Old Testament. Many Old Testament passages were read and explained to him. Jesus, along with the other boys his age, was required to memorize large portions of the Old Testament.

The only glimpse we have of his youth happened when he was twelve years old. That spring, when it was time for the Passover feast, Jesus was taken to Jerusalem to participate in the celebration.

This may have been his first time to see the holy city. As they approached the city, he saw the temple and was thrilled that soon he would go there. As he entered the court where Simeon had once held him and prophesied, he saw the altar with its smoking sacrifice. Glancing around, he saw the priests in their white robes, the Levites with their silver trumpets, and the teachers with their small groups of students. He was amazed at the beauty of the temple and the number of worshippers.

Each day of the feast was a special day as Jesus went to the temple area. He saw the priests and teachers and asked them about their duties. They answered his questions and saw that he clearly understood their replies. They were also amazed at how he could answer some of the questions they were discussing with their students. They were surprised that he had such a good understanding of the word of God.

On the day Jesus was to leave for Nazareth, he went one more time to the temple and began to talk to the priests. Time passed quickly and soon it was evening. Joseph and Mary had started for Nazareth early that afternoon. They thought Jesus was with the other children in the group of people with whom they were traveling. But when evening came, they could not find him. They were alarmed and began to search for him. Their search led them back to Jerusalem where they asked their friends and relatives if they had seen him. No one had. Finally, after three days of searching, they went to the temple area to pray. There they found their son sitting with the priests and teachers, listening to them and answering their questions. Mary, relieved that they had found him, asked him why he had stayed and caused them so much anxiety. His answer was one that she would think about for a long time. He told her that he must be in his Father's house teaching about his Father. His reply made a deep impression on Mary. She thought about it often as she recalled to mind his birth, the shepherds, the wise men, and the many prophesies that had been fulfilled.

Jesus then obeyed his parents, and they went home to Nazareth. Jesus grew from a boy to a young man. He grew in knowledge, wisdom, and in the fear of God. Possibly he learned the trade of a carpenter. And so, in a carpenter shop in a quiet city, the years passed until Jesus was thirty. At that time John, his forerunner, introduced him to the nation of Israel, and he began his public ministry.

Questions for Discussion

1. The Passover feast was a celebration. What were they celebrating?
2. What questions do you think Jesus asked the teachers in the temple?
3. What questions do you think the teachers asked Jesus?
4. What did Jesus mean when he said he must be in his Father's house doing his Father's will?
5. What do you think Jesus was like as he was growing up?
6. Jesus grew in knowledge, wisdom, and the fear of the Lord. What can we do so that we can grow in the same way?

Summary Note

The story of the birth of Christ and all the events that happened is very interesting and amazing. Many Old Testament prophecies were fulfilled during this time. Many surprising events took place. Who can forget the angelic appearances, the virgin birth, the shepherds, or the wise men and their worship? But what is even more amazing is what Christ did after John introduced him to the nation of Israel. He became a healer, a teacher, a miracle worker, the crucified Savior, and the risen Lord.

DECEMBER 23 | The Child Becomes a Man

John 1:19-29 |Now this was John's testimony when the Jewish leaders in Jerusalem sent priests and Levites to ask him who he was. He did not fail to confess, but confessed freely, "I am not the Messiah."

They asked him, "Then who are you? Are you Elijah?"

He said, "I am not."

"Are you the Prophet?"

He answered, "No."

Finally they said, "Who are you? Give us an answer to take back to those who sent us. What do you say about yourself?"

John replied in the words of Isaiah the prophet, "I am the voice of one calling in the wilderness, 'Make straight the way for the Lord.'"

Now the Pharisees who had been sent questioned him, "Why then do you baptize if you are not the Messiah, nor Elijah, nor the Prophet?"

"I baptize with water," John replied, "but among you stands one you do not know. He is the one who comes after me, the straps of whose sandals I am not worthy to untie."

This all happened at Bethany on the other side of the Jordan, where John was baptizing.

John 1:34 |The next day John saw Jesus coming toward him and said, "Look, the Lamb of God, who takes away the sin of the world! ...I have seen and I testify that this is God's Chosen One."

Thirty years had passed since John and Jesus had been born. Both of them now began their ministries to the people of Israel. John became well known to the people before Jesus did. It had been prophesied that John would be the forerunner of Christ. He was to tell the people who Jesus was.

When John first appeared, his message to the people was that they should repent of their sins. He told them that the kingdom of heaven was going to come soon. After hearing his message, many of the people asked John if he was the Christ, the Savior of Israel. He told them that he was a voice crying in the wilderness, "Prepare the way of the Lord." He told them that there was one coming whose shoe he was not even worthy to untie. He told them that he was going to introduce them to the Savior.

One day as John was talking to some of his followers, Jesus Christ came walking up the road. John immediately pointed to him and said, "Look, the Lamb of God, who takes away the sin of the world." John again told them of the mission of Christ and how he would save them from their sins.

Jesus, after being baptized by John, began his ministry to the people. He told them who he was and what he would do. He began his ministry by teaching the people about the Old Testament law. He told them how they could please God by obeying Him and living as the Scriptures said to live. Throughout his entire ministry he continually taught the people about his Father, salvation, and how to live a live pleasing to God.

Jesus also performed many miracles during his ministry. He changed water into wine, healed people who were sick or crippled, fed five thousand with five loaves of bread and two fish, and even raised people from the dead. He performed miracles when he was on the sea with his disciples. Once he walked on water. Another time he calmed the wind and the waves.

Jesus ministered on the earth about three and a half years. At the end of this time he became the crucified Savior. Jesus had come to the earth so that he could be the sacrifice for the sins of the world. This meant he had to die. He told his disciples that he would die, but they didn't understand. One night he was arrested in a garden where he was praying. He was put on trial and convicted of speaking against God. He had told the truth: he was the son of God. For this he was going to be killed. After determining that he was guilty, he was taken to a place called Calvary where he was crucified along with two thieves. There Jesus died as an offering for the sins of the world (see Romans 3:1-4). After Jesus was dead, he was taken down from the cross and buried in a borrowed tomb.

However, the story doesn't end there! Three days after he was buried some women came to his tomb so that they could prepare his body for a proper burial. To their great surprise and amazement, he was not there. They couldn't believe it! They thought someone had stolen his body. Jesus, knowing their thoughts and feelings of helplessness, appeared to them and told them that he had been raised from the dead. He was alive! This showed that he was indeed who he said he was: the son of God. He had risen from the dead so that his people could have salvation. He had died as a sacrifice and risen as their king.

Questions for Discussion

1. Why did the people think John was the Christ?
2. What did John mean when he said he was not worthy to untie Jesus' shoe?
3. What does it mean to repent of your sin?
4. What does it mean that Jesus is the Lamb of God?
5. Jesus died for the sins of the world. Do you believe that he died to pay for your sins?
6. Jesus rose from the grave as a king. Will you let him be the ruler in your life?

Summary Note

Now the Christmas story is complete. The baby who had been born in a manger was going back to heaven to live with his Father. He had been gone a long time. Jesus had come to the earth, lived as a man, died as a sacrifice, and rose again as a king. Like the wise men, let us remember to praise and worship him as we celebrate Christmas this year.

(Perhaps these two passages could be done as a choral reading. Perhaps the oldest member of the family could read it. Read the Scriptures and discuss the questions; there is no narrative.)

Luke 2:1-20 | In those days Caesar Augustus issued a decree that a census should be taken of the entire Roman world. (This was the first census that took place while Quirinius was governor of Syria.) And everyone went to their own town to register.

So Joseph also went up from the town of Nazareth in Galilee to Judea, to Bethlehem the town of David, because he belonged to the house and line of David. He went there to register with Mary, who was pledged to be married to him and was expecting a child. While they were there, the time came for the baby to be born, and she gave birth to her firstborn, a son. She wrapped him in cloths and placed him in a manger, because there was no guest room available for them.

And there were shepherds living out in the fields nearby, keeping watch over their flocks at night. An angel of the Lord appeared to them, and the glory of the Lord shone around them, and they were terrified. But the angel said to them, "Do not be afraid. I bring you good news that will cause great joy for all the people. Today in the town of David a Savior has been born to you; he is the Messiah, the Lord. This will be a sign to you: You will find a baby wrapped in cloths and lying in a manger."

Suddenly a great company of the heavenly host appeared with the angel, praising God and saying,

"Glory to God in the highest heaven,

and on earth peace to those on whom his favor rests."

When the angels had left them and gone into heaven, the shepherds said to one another, "Let's go to Bethlehem and see this thing that has happened, which the Lord has told us about."

So they hurried off and found Mary and Joseph, and the baby, who was lying in the manger. When they had seen him, they spread the word concerning what had been told them about this child, and all who heard it were amazed at what the shepherds said to them. But Mary treasured up all these things and pondered them in her heart. The shepherds returned, glorifying and praising God for all the things they had heard and seen, which were just as they had been told.

Matthew 2:1-12 | After Jesus was born in Bethlehem in Judea, during the time of King Herod, Magi from the east came to Jerusalem and asked, "Where is the one who has been born king of the Jews? We saw his star when it rose and have come to worship him."

When King Herod heard this he was disturbed, and all Jerusalem with him. When he had called together all the people's chief priests and teachers of the law, he asked them where the Messiah was to be born. "In Bethlehem in Judea," they replied, "for this is what the prophet has written:

"'But you, Bethlehem, in the land of Judah,
are by no means least among the rulers of Judah;
for out of you will come a ruler
who will shepherd my people Israel.'"

Then Herod called the Magi secretly and found out from them the exact time the star had appeared. He sent them to Bethlehem and said, "Go and search carefully for the child. As soon as you find him, report to me, so that I too may go and worship him."

After they had heard the king, they went on their way, and the star they had seen when it rose went ahead of them until it stopped over the place where the child was. When they saw the star, they were overjoyed. On coming to the house, they saw the child with his mother Mary, and they bowed down and worshiped him. Then they opened their treasures and presented him with gifts of gold, frankincense and myrrh. And having been warned in a dream not to go back to Herod, they returned to their country by another route.

Luke 1:37 | For nothing is impossible with God (NLT).

Questions for Discussion

1. What do you think is the most unbelievable part of the Christmas story?
2. What do you think is the most interesting part of the Christmas story?
3. Do you really believe that with God nothing is impossible?

Summary Note

The Christmas story is truly an unforgettable and unbelievable story. Who can forget the angelic appearances, the place of his birth, the shepherds, the wise men, or even the evil King Herod? In turn, who can believe the story that God came to this earth as a baby? Who can believe the story that this baby came to be the payment for the sins of the world? We all can, because the Bible teaches us that nothing is impossible with God. We can believe what the Bible says.

DECEMBER 25 | A Christmas Prayer

Matthew 1:18-25 | This is how the birth of Jesus the Messiah came about: His mother Mary was pledged to be married to Joseph, but before they came together, she was found to be pregnant through the Holy Spirit. Because Joseph her husband was faithful to the law, and yet did not want to expose her to public disgrace, he had in mind to divorce her quietly.

But after he had considered this, an angel of the Lord appeared to him in a dream and said, "Joseph son of David, do not be afraid to take Mary home as your wife, because what is conceived in her is from the Holy Spirit. She will give birth to a son, and you are to give him the name Jesus, because he will save his people from their sins."

All this took place to fulfill what the Lord had said through the prophet: "The virgin will conceive and give birth to a son, and they will call him Immanuel" (which means "God with us").

When Joseph woke up, he did what the angel of the Lord had commanded him and took Mary home as his wife. But he did not consummate their marriage until she gave birth to a son. And he gave him the name Jesus.

A Christmas Prayer

Dear God,

Thank you for your son. Through him we know your love and truth. We are amazed just as the shepherds were that you sent him to this earth.

We remember that even though he was laid in a manger, one day he will be the king of all heaven and earth. Like the wise men, we seek to worship him and give him our best.

Help us to remember that Christmas is more than just a time of decorations and gifts. Help us to understand that it is above all a time to celebrate your son's coming to this earth to save sinners. Like Mary, we want to treasure this in our hearts and remember it all year long.

Thank you for the greatest gift ever given. Thank you for showing us your love and grace. Thank you for sending your Spirit, who has given us new life. Like Joseph, we desire to be obedient and be guided by your hand.

Like Jesus, help us to love others with our lives.

We love you! Amen.

BEFORE

Before   the beautiful melodies of a Christmas choir,
          there was "A Silent Night."

Before tinsel was strung on a tree,
          there were millions of stars strung throughout the
          sky to light the plains for the first nativity.

Before a child's eyes were filled with wonder by the
presents under a tree,
          there was the wonder of the virgin birth.

Before a tree was ever topped with a beautiful angel,
          there was a heavenly band of angels watching over
          the Bethlehem plains.

Before lights were strung on a tree,
          there was a single guiding star lighting up the
          birthplace of the Christ child.

Before choirs raised hymns of praise on a Christmas Eve,
          there was a heavenly choir singing "Glory to God in
          the Highest" to announce the birth of his son.

Before gifts were ever opened on a Christmas morning,
          wise men traveled far to give gifts to the newborn
          king.

Before greenery was ever woven to make an Advent
wreath,
          there was the birth of a King, the first advent of the
          Savior.

Richard A. Iles

Made in the USA
Lexington, KY
02 December 2019

58009242R00070